D1511930

Let's Learn to Ski

Walker and Company / New York

Gene and Barbara Tinker

Let's Learn to Ski

First published in the United States of America
in 1969 by Walker and Company, a division of the
Walker Publishing Company, Inc.

Published simultaneously in Canada by The Ryerson
Press, Toronto.

Library of Congress Catalog Card Number: 70-86408

Printed in the United States of America

Book designed by Lena Fong Lueg

To our children, David, Wendy, and Gena, with much love and gratitude for the many long hours they spent posing for these pictures

Thank you for your help . . .

This book could not have been written without the wholehearted assistance of several of our friends who are as interested in skiing as we are. Our editor, Tracy Tothill, encouraged us and gave us all the help we needed. At Big Bromley, Vermont, where the pictures were taken, Burr Vail, the manager, was generous with his time and advice. Ace Manley, the Bromley ski school director, offered suggestions and we are grateful for his help. The Garcia Company supplied Fischer skis, Marker bindings, Humanic boots, and Uvex goggles. The Spinnerin Corporation enabled our models to dress in the latest in ski wear.

Table of Contents

6

Introduction

Skiing is fun. Almost anyone who is in good health can enjoy the exciting feeling of flying smoothly down a snow-covered mountain. Skiing is a sport that is enjoyed in one of Nature's most beautiful and healthy settings, the mountains—where lovely scenery and crisp, clean air make you feel alive and healthy.

Skiing means speed—speed that you control. It is speed unlike the kind you find in a car or a boat, even on a jet airplane. Because you are so close to the snow-covered surface of the mountain, even a speed of a few miles an hour can be thrilling.

You will enjoy your sport much more if you remember that skiing *is* a sport, something you do for fun. The skiers who have the most fun are those who do not get angry at themselves when they fall down and who take plenty of time to practice each lesson before trying to learn the next step. Don't feel that you must learn all there is to know in one or two days. You can't and will just end up feeling angry at yourself. Relax and enjoy your new sport. Remember, skiing is for *fun* and there is nothing to prove by skiing when it is too cold, or you are too tired or angry at falling down. If you are tired or don't feel well, skip your lesson or day of skiing until you feel better.

One of the wonderful things about skiing is that you can learn at your own pace. However soon you learn the various steps in

skiing, you know that you alone have mastered each ski slope you use and you alone have learned each step toward becoming a good skier.

In several other sports, you play with or against someone else and you can really enjoy these sports only if you and the ones you play with have about the same ability. In tennis, for example, if one of the players is much better at the game than the other, neither of you will enjoy the match very much. This is not so in skiing—except in racing. How quickly you learn and how fast you ski is up to you. You can go at your own speed.

Some skiers find a lot of fun on gentle novice slopes while others use the steeper trails. The slope that is just right for you is the one which you can use safely and gives you the most pleasure.

Skiing can be enjoyed equally by all members of your family. You can have a day's fun on the ski slopes with your parents, relatives, or friends no matter how much older they may be. In fact, adults have found that many children learn faster than they do. Skiing is also a sport in which girls can do just as well as boys.

Who can ski? Anyone who is in good health. When you go to a ski area you will see men, women, boys, and girls having a wonderful time. While some children have learned to ski when very young, most children begin when they are six years old, or older. At six, most children are usually able to control their skis and safely use the uphill lifts.

Where Can You Ski?

Where can you ski? Anywhere there is a snow-covered hill. Not too long ago, skiers had to be pretty tough. There were no ski lifts up the mountain. Skiers had to walk uphill.

Now, most skiing is done at ski areas where you are taken uphill by machines. There are ski areas in many parts of our country. Snow-making machines make it possible to have skiing almost anywhere, even in some of our Southern states. All that is needed is below-freezing weather. Many ski areas offer night skiing. Huge floodlights light up the slopes.

Ski slopes are marked to show how steep they are and how hard it is to use them. Usually, they are marked "less difficult," "average," or "more difficult." It is best to learn how a slope is marked before you try it. If you are a beginner, it would be better to try a gentle hill.

You will find that no two trips down the same trail will be the same. Snow conditions change, ice forms or melts, and bumps (moguls) appear or change in size. You can enjoy skiing the same slope many times, although most ski areas have several slopes for each kind of skier, novice through expert.

Several ski areas give lessons each week to children from

3

Skiers go through a "snowstorm" caused by snow-making machines at Big Bromley, Vermont, which has the world's largest system of snow-making equipment.

nearby schools. These lessons are for children who ski just for the fun of it as well as for those who race. At one such ski area, Big Bromley, in Vermont, many schoolchildren take lessons each week. Many of these young skiers become fine racers. Others just have a great time skiing for fun.

Different Kinds of Skiing

There are two kinds of skiing: Alpine and Nordic. Alpine skiing began in the Austrian, Swiss, and French Alps of Europe. Alpine skiers (sometimes called downhill skiers) use heavy, stiff boots, bindings that fasten the boots tightly to the skis, stiff skis with steel edges, and strong metal poles. The Alpine skier uses lifts to go up a mountain, then skis more or less straight down.

4

Nordic skiing is divided into two activities: cross-country skiing and ski jumping. Cross-country skiers use lightweight bindings, boots, and poles, and light, narrow skis. They enjoy exploring the backwoods areas far from the downhill ski slopes. The ski jumper is a specialist. He uses special skis and practices to see how far and how gracefully he can jump after sliding down a long, steep, snow-covered jumping ramp.

This book will help you to learn Alpine skiing. So far, it is the most popular kind of skiing in this country.

To nonskiers our sport might seem fairly dangerous. This is not at all true. Skiing is as safe as you make it. Learn proper skiing methods, have proper equipment, ski in control (be able to turn and stop whenever you want to), and use your common sense—and skiing will be far safer than many other sports. At first, even the gentlest novice slope will seem rather steep to you, and you will need practice to get used to the equipment you use. However, if you study the following pages, take lessons from a professional instructor, and practice, practice, practice, you will soon be having the time of your life on the ski slopes. Practice is necessary—and luckily skiing practice, unlike other kinds of practice, is fun.

There is no thrill quite like the one you feel when you master a slope that seemed difficult at first. And few sports give you the feeling of joy and freedom that you get when you ski smoothly and at your own speed down a ski slope.

1

Skiing Equipment

You will always remember your first day of skiing. Even after you become an expert you will remember the first thrill of gliding across the snow on skis. It is important to make sure that your first experience is a good one. This chapter will help you to choose equipment that is just right for you—and this will give you a big boost toward becoming a good skier.

How to Choose Your Equipment

Before you can learn to ski you must have at least the following items: skis, bindings, boots, poles, and warm clothing. If you have the right equipment, skiing will be easy to learn.

What is the "right" equipment? It is equipment that fits well and comfortably, is the proper size, and is made especially for your age, height, weight, and skiing ability. Making the right choice is easy when you know what to look for.

Renting Equipment

Many beginners rent equipment the first time or two they go skiing. By renting gear you can find out just how well you like the sport before buying your own equipment. Renting equipment also allows you to try out different types and brands of equipment to see which you like best.

Where to Find a Rental Shop: Rental shops are found in and near ski areas, in some sporting-goods stores, and in ski shops in some large cities. You will find that the men in the rental shop will take as much time as they can to make sure that you get good equipment of the right size. They want you to return again and again to skiing—and to their store, of course!

How to Choose Rental Equipment: Don't try to rent equipment by yourself. An experienced skier should help you.

Since your parents are paying for the use of rental gear, you have the right to make sure it is in good condition. You can't expect to rent brand-new skis, boots, and poles from a rental shop. You can expect, though, to find skis that aren't warped, cracked, or broken; bindings that work properly and are adjusted to fit your boots; poles that are not bent and that have baskets and straps in good condition; and boots that fit correctly and are not cracked, warped, or too soft. The rest of this chapter tells you how to choose new equipment. Our comments on what to look for in new equipment also apply to rentals.

Buying Equipment

One of the first things you will notice when you go to a ski shop is the many different kinds of equipment for sale. Skis are made of wood, metal, and fiberglass. Boots are made of rubber, leather, and leather/plastic combinations. Bindings come in many styles and shapes. Even poles differ greatly from brand to brand. It may be hard at first to be sure which is the best gear for you, until you learn what to look for.

There is a good reason for the different kinds of equipment. Skiing is enjoyed by people of all sizes, shapes, and ages. It would be impossible, for example, for you to ski well on your father's skis, or he on yours. There must be many kinds of equipment to fit the many different people who ski.

There are a few things to keep in mind when you buy:

First, the best place to buy equipment is from a professional ski shop. They will usually have many varieties to choose from. You will find ski shops at ski areas and in cities. Most of the people who work in these shops are skiers themselves and can help you greatly. You can also buy gear from the sporting-goods departments of some department stores, from some sports shops, even by mail order. If you buy from these places, it is especially important to get advice from an expert skier.

Second, choose what is best for *you*. Too many beginners buy a certain brand or type of skis or boots because they see a ski instructor or famous racer wear that particular brand. As a beginner, you will need equipment that is quite different from that used by advanced skiers. It doesn't make much sense to buy anything just because a famous person does.

Third, take your time in choosing equipment. Don't try to do it in a hurry. You could make a mistake by rushing. Be choosy.

Fourth, if you can't spend too much money, do *not* try to save on your boots by buying a cheap variety or a pair of soft, worn-out used boots. Boots are the most important item you will buy. Your boots control your skis. If your boots do not fit right, you cannot control them, and if you cannot control your boots and skis, you will find it very hard to learn to ski. You don't need to get the highest-priced boots you can find, but you should make sure you have boots of good quality.

Skis

Skis are long strips of wood, metal, or fiberglass. They come in pairs, one for each foot. They vary in length from two and a half feet or less to about seven feet. Their shape depends on the type of skiing they are designed for. They are usually widest near the front and narrowest at the middle. They are pointed and

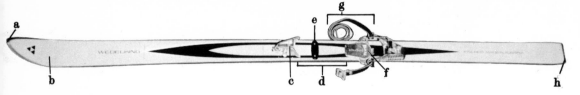

(a) Tip; (b) Shovel; (c) Toe Piece; (d) Waist; (e) Boot Plate;
(f) Heel Piece; (g) Arlberg Strap; (h) Tail

curve up at the front end. The photo shows you the names for the various parts of the ski.

Cost: Children's skis cost from $20.00 or less to $50.00 or more. The more you pay, the better will be the quality of your skis. However, some experts say that it is best to buy the less costly wooden skis, because children grow so fast they usually outgrow a pair of skis in a year or two.

Others say that the beginner should start with the very best equipment because beginners need all the help they can get. These experts advise spending up to $70.00 for the top-quality Fischer Silverglass Senator Youth fiberglass skis, or the $95.00 Wedelking Youth metal skis.

How Long Will They Last? How long your skis last depends on several things: how often you use them, how "hard" you ski, and how you take care of them. A pair of good wooden skis will usually last two or more ski seasons. Wooden skis need more care than fiberglass or metal skis. However, many skiers have used them for years.

Metal and fiberglass skis last a long time, probably longer than you will be able to use them—that is, you will probably outgrow them before you wear them out.

Since metal skis last so long, they usually have a high trade-in value when it is time for you to get a longer pair. You may get as much as half the cost back when you trade in.

Choosing the Right Length: For years, most skiers felt that the right length for skis was about a foot longer than the height of

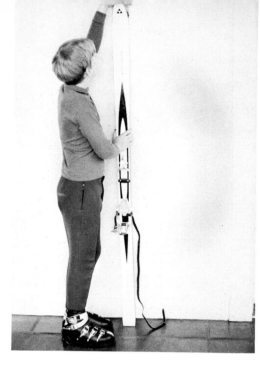

If you are a good skier, you can use a ski about a foot longer than your height. One way of measuring ski height is to stand straight, holding your arm above your head. The ski tip will just reach the base of your hand, as shown here. When you are just beginning, it will be easier to learn on a shorter ski— one that is about your height or an inch or two longer.

the skier. Thus, if you were four feet tall, you would use a five-foot ski. Another way to get about the same result would be to use a ski that just reaches the base of your hand when you stand straight with your arm held above your head.

Many experts now feel that it is better to start with shorter skis, ones that are about the same as the skier's height. Turning is easier with these shorter skis.

Still other experts use skis of different lengths in teaching. The student begins on very short skis. As his skiing improves, he uses longer and longer skis until he is using skis six to twelve inches longer than his height. This is the Graduated Length Method of teaching.

Although not all the experts agree about the best length for beginner's skis, some things are agreed upon:

1. It is easier to learn on shorter skis (the length of the skier's height, or shorter) than on long skis.
2. Once the beginner becomes a good enough skier to ski fast, longer skis are better. Short skis do not "track" well. That is, when you ski fast, it is harder to make them go in a straight line than it is with the longer ones.

3. Age, weight, and how well you ski are important. Teen-agers and adults can manage longer skis more easily than children. A heavier skier can use a longer ski than a lighter person. As you improve, you may do better with longer skis. If you learn skiing through the Graduated Length Method, your instructor will tell you how long your skis should be, and will provide them while you are learning. Otherwise in the beginning choose a ski that is about the same length as your height.

Other Things You Should Know About Skis: Your skis must have sharp steel edges. Without them, you will not be able to turn properly.

Skis are made for a certain purpose. The racer would not use the same model as a beginner, for instance. Here are some of the more commonly used skis:

Standard: This is an all-around ski and is good for the beginner.

Combi (or Combination): Used by advanced beginners and intermediate skiers. It is somewhat stiffer than standards and is a good, all-purpose ski for the weekend skier.

Giant Slalom, Slalom, and Downhill: Used by advanced skiers and by racers. Deep Powder skis are used for very soft, deep snow.

The bottoms of your skis should be of plastic (polyethylene). Older skis have painted-on bottoms. These bottoms have to be repainted and waxed often. It is far better to get skis that have a special hard plastic bottom such as P-Tex 2000. You will enjoy skiing more and will find them much easier to take care of than skis with painted bottoms.

If you place a ski on the floor you can see that it curves up, off the floor, in the center of the ski. This built-in curve is called "camber." You can tell how much camber is just right for you by standing on the ski. If your weight is just enough to make the entire bottom of the ski touch the floor, the ski has the right camber.

There will be a groove running along the bottoms of your skis. A shallow groove makes turning easy whereas a deep groove helps you to "track" straight down a hill. Of course, the groove will help

"Camber" is the curve built into your skis. When you step on them, they should flatten out and distribute your weight equally throughout the length of the ski.

13

you only when you are on snow; when you run over a patch of ice, the ski bottoms cannot "bite" in and the groove is not of much help.

When you place your skis on the floor on their bottoms, the tips and tails should lie flat; there should be no twisting or warp of any kind.

Boots

Ski boots are made of leather, plastic, leather/plastic combinations, or rubber. They are laced or buckled. They should fit very snugly. Their purpose is to support your ankles and feet, to connect your feet to the skis, and to let you control your skis. As we said before, they are the most important item you will buy. Good boots make skiing easy—poor ones take all the fun out of your sport.

The cheaper rubber boots are sometimes used by small children. However, they do not give the support needed for good skiing and they do not "breathe." That is, they keep the dampness from perspiration inside the boots, which may make your feet get very cold. Also, they are not always padded as well as the other kinds, which also causes cold feet.

Ski boots are for skiing, not walking. Of course, a certain amount of walking is necessary but it is best to have a pair of after-ski boots handy. They will be more comfortable when relaxing at lunch or after skiing. Also, too much walking in ski boots makes them softer, which means less control over your skis.

Cost: Children's boots may cost from a few dollars for the cheap rubber kind to $55.00 or more for high-quality leather-and-plastic buckle boots such as Humanic boots. It is better to buy the very best boots your parents can afford. In any case, plan to spend at least $20.00 for boots. (Many ski shops have a special service for growing children—outgrown boots can be traded in for a pair that fits.)

Getting the Proper Fit: When you have properly fitted boots on, they will feel much different from hunting boots or your regular shoes. Ski boots differ from other kinds of footwear in the way they are made and in the way they fit. If at all possible, be sure to buy your boots at a professional ski shop. The people there will help you find the boots that are just right for you.

All of the inside surface of the boot should be in contact with your foot. The boots should feel very snug but not so tight they hurt. A cup or socket is built into the boot where your heel is. Make sure your heel fits snugly into this socket—otherwise, the boots will not feel right even though they may be the right size. See the next section on how to put them on.

Do not buy boots in a hurry. Take your time. Try on several pairs to see how different sizes and brands feel on your feet. Be sure to try on both boots, not just one. Be sure that you can wiggle your toes. If you can't, the boots are too tight.

Leather stretches because of dampness and the strain placed on it when skiing. For this reason, it is better to get a pair of boots that are very snug when new rather than a pair that fits too comfortably, like a pair of old shoes.

If you buy your boots in a pro ski shop where you will be fitted by an experienced skier, you can be sure that you will be shown boots of good quality.

How to Put on Ski Boots: It is important to put on your boots the proper way so they will fit just right. Be sure to wear your stretch pants and a pair of heavy wool socks over a thin pair when putting on boots. Lace boots are put on differently from buckle boots as illustrated in the pictures.

Buckle boots are easier and quicker to put on and take off than lace boots. Many skiers loosen their buckles after they get on the chairlift to increase blood circulation, which warms their feet. They tighten the buckles again before skiing.

Whether you use lace or buckle boots, it is important that they let you bend your knees. Here's how to find out if you can bend

Here's how to put on lace boots:
After you've loosened the laces,
slide your foot in, making sure
your socks aren't wrinkled.

Now, kick your heel sharply on the
floor. This will make your heel fit
into the built-in heel cup at the
back of your boot.

Lace up the inner boot—snugly
but not too tight.

Then, lace up the outer boot. Put
on the other boot the same way.
Stand up and take a few steps.
The boots should feel very snug,
but there should be no pain on any
part of your feet. If the boots hurt
your feet, try on a different pair of
boots.

Here's how to put on buckle boots: Open all the buckles and pull out the tongue. Put your foot in the boot. Make sure your socks do not wrinkle.

Kick your heel sharply on the floor to fit your heel into the heel cup.

Buckle the first three or four buckles at the loosest settings. Crouch with your boot sole flat on the floor and push your knee forward. This will set your heel into the heel cup in the boot. Next, set the buckles to a tighter notch and push your knee forward again to make sure that your heel is properly placed in the boot.

Finally, set the buckles for a very snug fit. Do the same with the other boot.

them enough. With your boots on, stand up, then bend your knees forward, keeping the soles of your boots flat on the floor. You should be able to bend your knees so that they are about even with the tip of your boots. At first, you may have to leave the top buckle on a loose setting to permit enough forward lean. Without enough forward lean, you will not be able to ski well and you could hurt yourself in a fall.

Bindings

What They Are: Bindings are metal devices that fasten your ski boots to your skis. They are made to hold your skis on when you ski and to release when you fall. For this reason, they are called release bindings. It is quite important to have release bindings that are put on right and properly adjusted to make sure that they release when they should, and not before or after. It is also important to get bindings that are made especially for children.

Premounted Bindings: Some skis, usually the cheaper ones, are sold with bindings already on them. If you buy this kind, make sure that the bindings are adjusted so they will release at the right time. The release settings will depend on your height, weight, and skiing ability.

Types of Unmounted Bindings: Better skis are usually sold without bindings. The problem, then, is to get a pair of bindings and have them mounted in the right place on your skis. Here are a few things you will want to know about these bindings.

There are three general types of bindings: cable, step-in, and latch-in. Cable bindings have been used for many years. They have a toe piece and a cable that goes back along the sides of the ski and fits around the heel groove of your boot.

Step-in and latch-in bindings are fairly new and are used more and more because usually they will release no matter which way you fall. They are also easier to put on and take off.

Which Kind Should You Get? Most bindings now on the market are good; however, many experts feel that the latch-in and step-in varieties are better and safer than cable bindings. Usually, the more you pay for bindings the better they are. Many experts feel that the latch-in Marker bindings shown in the pictures throughout the book are the best of their type.

Mounting Your Bindings: Bindings must be mounted in exactly the right spot on your skis. Have this job done by an expert. If the bindings are incorrectly mounted, you will not be able to ski as well as you should.

Checkups and Adjustments: Bindings should be checked by an expert every once in a while to make sure they still work properly. If they release too easily or not at all, take them to a ski shop for a checkup right away. Also, be sure to have them checked at the beginning of the ski season.

Runaway Straps: Runaway straps are strips of leather attached to your bindings. They prevent your skis from sliding downhill when your bindings release. The best one is the Arlberg strap.

Poles

What They Are: Ski poles are used in several ways to help you ski. The shafts are made of aluminum or steel. They have a rubber or plastic handle with a strap at one end and a "basket" at the other, pointed, end. The basket keeps the pole from sinking too far into soft snow. The strap helps you to use your poles and keeps them from slipping out of your hands.

How to Choose Poles: Poles should be light and should feel comfortable in your hands. They should not feel heavy at the basket end. Try several pairs in the ski shop before you buy. Swing them forward and back a few times to get their "feel" and make sure they feel comfortable while handling them. The straps should be long enough for you to use them easily with gloves or mittens. The pictures on this page show how to put your hands into the pole straps.

To hold your ski poles correctly, first put your hand into the strap as shown. Be sure that the strap is not folded over and that it is placed around your wrist in a comfortable position.

Next, grip the handle of the pole as shown.

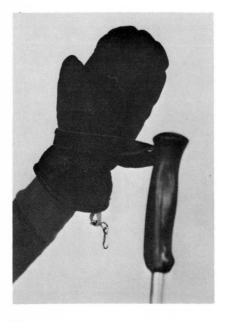

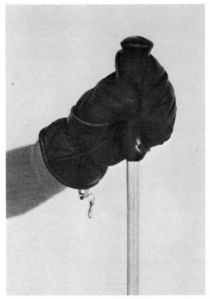

Choosing the Proper Length: Stand up straight with a pole placed under your arm, as shown in the picture. The handle of the pole should reach to an inch or two below your armpit.

If your poles are too short or too long, it will be hard to ski correctly. You will be leaning too far forward or backward and will have trouble keeping your balance.

Here's how to choose a set of poles of the right length. Stand straight and hold your arm out, as shown. The handle of the pole should reach to within an inch or two of your armpit.

Clothing

Ski clothing must keep you warm in a variety of situations: when you are sitting still on a chairlift, when you are skiing fast down a slope, and when you are walking or skating on the level. It is not as easy as it might seem to stay comfortable. For instance, when you get on the chairlift you might be very warm, even sweaty, from a fast run down the hill. Unless you're properly dressed, you might easily become chilled as you ride back uphill in the chair.

Your ski clothes must keep the heat of your body in and keep the cold weather out. It will be easier to keep warm if you wear several layers of thin clothing rather than one heavy layer.

Color: You may choose whatever colors you like, but it is worth knowing that darker colors will usually not show stains or streaks that sometimes come from hard wear.

Pants: Ski pants should be comfortable and roomy or stretchy enough to allow you to move your body freely in any direction. They should also be water-repellent. They have a strap that goes around the arch of your foot—this keeps the pants from pulling up on your leg and letting in the snow. The warmest pants are of wool and a stretch cloth such as the Spinnerin pants shown in the pictures in this book. Pockets should have zippers.

Parka: A parka should also be roomy, comfortable, and water-resistant. Some parkas, called shells, are thin, unlined, nylon jackets. They are worn over sweaters. Other parkas are quilted or padded, and are very warm. Some parkas have a built-in hood that zips into a pouch in the collar. Hoods are useful on cold, windy, snowy days. Pockets should have zippers.

It is usually best to wear your parka over your sweaters except for warm, spring skiing. The closely woven, water-resistant outer surface of the parka will keep the wind out and your body heat in. It will also keep you from getting wet when you fall.

Caps and Headbands: On mild days, you can wear a headband, as shown in the picture. These are inexpensive and they keep your ears warm. During cold days, you will need a cap, or hat. The warmest kind are those of heavy wool.

Some skiers wear masks. They are of wool or leather. These masks help to keep your face warm and are useful when the wind blows. However, they may be hard to use if you wear glasses.

Underwear: One thing that you must have is long underwear, and it must fit snugly, neither too loose nor too tight. For skiing in very cold weather, you might want to wear two pairs of long underwear pants. Woolen underwear is very warm.

Sweaters: It is better to wear two or more fairly thin ones rather than one heavy sweater. The number of sweaters you wear will depend on how cold it is, how active you are, and how heavy your parka is. Wool sweaters are the warmest.

Headbands can be worn on mild days. They just keep your ears warm. On cold days, it is better to wear a hat.

Gloves or Mittens: Mittens are usually warmer than gloves. Some gloves, which are rather expensive, are said to be as warm as mittens. Whichever you choose, be sure that they repel water and are padded for cold weather. While skiing or riding the chairlift, you can warm your hands if they get cold by wiggling your fingers or by swinging your arms around in a circle. This makes your blood circulate faster, which helps to keep your hands warm.

Socks: Most skiers use a pair of thin socks, then put on a pair of heavy wool socks. Do not think that using two or more pairs of heavy socks will keep your feet warmer. If your boots fit properly —that is, tightly—another pair of stocks will cut off the blood circulation in your feet, which will make your feet cold.

Very Cold, Windy Weather: However cold it may be, it will seem to be much colder if the wind is blowing. When skiing on windy days, be sure that you do not stay outside too long. Always ski with a friend and check each other for frostbite. If you have frostbite, you will feel warm (at the frostbitten spot) where you at first felt cold. White spots on your skin are a sign of frostbite. Do not rub the frostbitten spot. Cover it with a glove or a scarf. Get into a warm room right away. When you once again have a tingling feeling where the frostbite was, you will be all right. If you are not sure you have recovered from frostbite, see a doctor. On very cold days, the ski patrolmen and lift attendants watch skiers very carefully for signs of frostbite. Be sure to do what they tell you to do.

Goggles: Skiers use goggles to protect their eyes from glare, wind, and blowing snow. Most goggles come with two sets of lenses: green and yellow, such as the Uvex goggles shown in the pictures. The green lenses are for skiing in bright sunshine. They are like sunglasses. Yellow lenses are worn when the sky is overcast and the light is "flat." In flat light, it is hard to see bumps on the slope. Yellow lenses make it easier to see these bumps. If you wear glasses, be sure that the goggles you buy can be fitted over the frames of your glasses.

Equipment Lock: It is a good idea to have a ski equipment lock. Some skiers have discovered that their skis and poles were taken from the outside ski racks while they were inside the base lodge warming up or having lunch. The most popular type of lock is a steel cable with a built-in lock. While you ski, you can wear it around your waist or over your shoulder and under your arm. Each time you take off your skis and go inside, run the cable through your ski bindings, around your skis, through the baskets of your poles and loop the cable around the ski rack to lock your equipment to the rack.

If you do not have a lock, you can separate your skis. Put a ski and a pole together in one spot, then take the other ski and pole to a different place. Just be sure to remember where you put everything!

2

Getting Started on Skis

The feeling of floating down a snow-covered hill is one you will enjoy again and again while skiing. Speed is important, but not at the very beginning. Before you can expect to handle even a beginner's slope, it is a good idea to learn a few things about yourself and your equipment and how to control your speed and direction while skiing downhill.

We know how to do many things, such as walk and sleep, without learning from books or going to school. We do them without even thinking about *how* we do them. Skiing is different. It is a sport that can be learned properly only by being taught. You shouldn't expect to ski like an expert the first time you put on skis any more than you should expect to play football like a pro the first time you have a ball in your hands. Happily, skiing is not hard to learn. In this chapter you will learn some of the beginning skiing maneuvers.

This book will help you learn to ski easily and quickly. However, you will learn much more quickly if you also take lessons. Nothing can take the place of a professional ski instructor who is right at your side, showing you what you're doing wrong and how to do it right and helping you to get over bad skiing habits. Even expert skiers take lessons once in a while, just to make sure that they are skiing as well as they possibly can.

Remember that each person is different in how fast he learns sports. Some beginners learn the snowplow turn easily while others might find it harder to do. Have patience with yourself.

Because skiing is a wonderful outdoor sport, try to learn it with a relaxed, happy feeling. Don't be embarrassed when you fall. Everyone falls. Don't think that everyone is looking at you when you fall. The other skiers are so busy with their own skiing that they don't have time to think about how funny you look when you fall.

For your first few times on skis, you might get tired rather soon. When you do, stop. Relax. If you're cold, go into the lodge and get warm. Then ski for a while again. There is no hurry and you shouldn't feel that you *must* practice for hours and hours. You will learn a lot faster and have more fun if you take it easy.

Methods of Teaching Skiing

As this book is written, there are at least three methods of teaching skiing in this country: the American System, the Graduated Length Method, and the American Parallel Technique.

You might wonder which is best. The answer is that they are all good and they all work toward the same goal—to teach people to become parallel skiers and to make skiing fun. Those who teach, or were taught by, one or the other of these systems are sure that "their" system is best. In any case, the system used by your instructor will be whichever one is chosen by the ski area you visit and you will not really have a choice of methods, unless you go to a different ski area.

The instruction given in this book is closer to the American System than to the other two because it is the one most commonly used.

How to Carry Your Skis

There are various ways of carrying your skis, as shown in these pictures: over your shoulder, in your hand, and in or under your arms. When you carry them over your shoulders, be careful to point them upward to make sure they don't hit someone behind you. Carrying skis under your arm is useful in crowded areas because you will not be so likely to hit someone else.

Some skiers use rubber tabs to keep their skis together. These tabs do not cost much and keep your skis from "scissoring," which dulls the edges. Scissored skis are shown in the picture.

(Top) You can carry your skis and poles in a variety of ways, as shown here—from left to right: 1) over your shoulder with your poles over the other shoulder, helping to carry the weight of the skis; 2) under your arms, with skis and poles together; 3) in your arms; or 4) with the pole straps looped over the skis' tips and tails so you can carry them like a suitcase. (Lower left) If you carry your skis over your shoulder, be sure to keep the tips pointed upward. Otherwise, you might hit someone when you turn around. (Lower right) Skis are said to be "scissored" when they are crossed as shown here. Scissoring should be avoided because the rubbing together of edges dulls them.

How to Warm Up Before Skiing

It is a good idea to stretch your muscles and warm up a bit before beginning a day's skiing, especially when you are a little stiff from a long drive to the ski area. You will find that a few minutes of exercise will prepare your muscles for the workout they will get on the slopes.

Deep Knee Bends: Stand straight with your arms in front of you. Squat down, then stand up again, keeping your back straight. Repeat this five or more times.

The Twist: Stand straight with your legs apart and your arms straight out to each side. Twist at the waist so your upper body is facing to the left. Then swing your upper body clear around to the right. Repeat this five or more times.

High Step: Stand straight with your arms hanging at your sides. Lift one leg, with knee bent, as high as you can. Do the same with the other leg. Repeat five or more times.

How to Put on Your Skis and Poles

Although you were probably shown how to put on your skis by the shop that sold them to you, it might be a good idea for us to explain this again.

After you have put on your boots, as shown in Chapter One, take your skis and poles to a flat snowy area and place your skis down side by side. The buckles of your Arlberg straps (the runaway straps, if you use single straps) should be on the outsides.

Whether you use cable, latch-in, or step-in bindings, be sure that when your boots are fastened into your bindings, they are lined up exactly with your skis. That is, pretend there is a straight line running down the center of your skis through the center of your boots.

(a) Here are the easy steps in fastening your boots to your bindings. First, place the skis on the snow, side by side, with the buckles on your runaway straps on the outsides, away from each other. (b) Next, place the toe of your boot into the toe piece of the binding. Make sure your boot toe is exactly centered in the binding. (c) Place the roller on the heel piece into the heel groove of your boot. (d) Pull up on the heel piece to lock your boot into place. (e) Wrap the Arlberg strap around your boot and run it through the slit, as shown. (f) Buckle the strap. As you can see, the strap buckle is on the outside. If the buckles were on the inside, next to each other, they might hook onto each other while you were skiing and you would fall. Now the ski is fastened securely to your boot and you can repeat the process with the other ski and boot.

Position the toe of your boot in the binding toe piece, then:

Cable bindings: Place the cable in the cable groove in the heel of your boot. Push the front throw unit forward to tighten the cable.

Latch-in bindings: Put the heel assembly in place in the cable groove in your boot and lock into place.

Step-in bindings: Push your heel into the heel unit of your bindings.

Among other things, your bindings allow you to lean far forward without falling on your nose. You can prove to yourself just how well your bindings will support you: Stand up straight. Slowly lean forward. Keep your knees stiff so you are entirely supported by your boots and bindings. You can lean much further forward this way than you could without the help of your boots and bindings.

Remember, when putting on your pole straps do not twist the straps.

How to Stand on Skis

The picture shows you the best way to stand on skis. You can have a little game with your skiing partner to find out if you are both standing properly. Stand in the proper position, then have

Here's how to prove to yourself that your bindings will really support you when you lean forward. Keep your knees locked stiff and slowly lean forward, while keeping your body stiff as a board. Do this a few times to gain confidence in your skis and bindings. Then, when your instructor tells you to lean forward, you can do so without worrying about falling on your nose!

When you stand on skis, remember to keep your knees bent and lean forward. Your weight should be on the balls of your feet. Keep your skis a comfortable distance apart.

your partner give you a little shove in the chest to try to see if you will lose your balance. When you are standing properly, you can stay on your feet even when pushed fairly hard. Be sure your partner is a good friend, though. You wouldn't want to be pushed too hard!

You will probably see expert skiers skiing with their skis so close that they almost seem glued together. This is good form and looks flashy—it is called parallel skiing. You will find skiing easier to learn at first if you keep your skis a comfortable distance apart. Before long, you will no doubt be a parallel skier, too. At the beginning, though, keep your skis apart.

You can easily build up a sense of balance on skis if you spend your first few sessions on very small hills that are not too steep. From the very beginning, get into the habit of looking ahead, not down at your skis. If you know what is ahead of you—a small bump, or another skier, or a tree—you can change your body position to keep your balance when changing direction or skiing over bumps. Also, get into the habit of holding your arms away from your body and in front of you. This will help you to develop a good sense of balance.

You will hear instructors say, "Keep your weight on the down-hill ski." This is proper for skiing across the face of a slope. However, there will be times when you will have some weight on the uphill ski, or when you will shift your weight back a little, or when you will be leaning far forward. The reason for these shifts in weight and body position is to keep your balance. When you have

One good way of getting used to the motion of sliding across the snow on skis is to have someone pull you along a flat snow-covered surface for a while. This young skier has already learned to keep her knees bent.

Walking on skis is easy—it is a series of gliding motions. Bend your knees a little and lean forward. Slide the ski forward in a short, gliding motion.

Then do the same with the other ski. Keep your skis on the snow. You needn't lift them up.

a good sense of balance on skis, these weight shifts will be automatic and you will keep your weight no matter what the surface is like or how many bumps or other skiers are in your way.

How to Walk on Skis

Choose a flat, snow-covered surface for your first walk on skis. It should be away from crowds and fast-moving skiers. If you have a snow-covered backyard, it will do fine. The pictures show you how to walk on skis.

You can use your poles to help you walk. Each time you take a step, push the opposite pole into the snow with your hand ahead of your body and your pole tip about even with your forward boot. This helps you to keep your balance. If you keep your pole pointed back, you can use it to give a little push to help yourself along.

As we said before, falling is a part of skiing. The important thing is not whether you fall, but that you learn how to fall and get up.

An easy way to learn to fall and get up is to practice. From a standing position on a flat, snow-covered surface, fall slightly backward and to one side, as shown in the picture. Use a hand to take up the shock of falling. Relax. Try not to stiffen up. Keep your eyes open. Try to keep your skis together. Hold your free

All skiers fall. The important thing is to learn to fall properly as shown here. Fall to one side, holding your uphill hand out to take up the shock of falling. Keep your ski poles pointed away from you.

To get up, bring your feet up close to your hips, then stick both poles in the snow as shown. Use your poles to push yourself up onto your feet.

hand out and in front of you to make sure you don't get hurt by your poles.

Bring your skis up close to your bottom and place them so they are close together and pointing in the same direction (parallel). Take off your pole straps. Hold both poles together and stick the baskets in the snow close behind you. Push yourself up by using your poles.

If you fall on a hill, move your skis so they are *below* you, or on the downhill side. Place them so they lie across the slope. If they are pointed uphill or downhill, you will slide downhill as soon as you put weight on them. Stamp your skis into the snow, hard, a few times before getting up. This makes a firm base to stand on.

A step turn can be used to change your direction while on a level, snow-covered surface.

How to Make a Step Turn

A step turn is used to turn around on a flat surface. Bend your knees slightly and lean forward. Lift up the tip of one ski and move it a few inches in the direction you want to go. Bring the other ski tip next to it. Leave the tails in place. Repeat this until you are headed in the right direction. Take small steps. Taking wide steps might make you cross your skis and fall.

How to Make a Kick Turn

A kick turn is used both on a flat surface and on a hill. It is quicker than the step turn. It can be used if you should find yourself on a hill too steep for you to make a skiing turn. It will be best to try this turn after you have skied a few times and are used to handling skis and being on them.

Stand on a flat surface and twist your upper body in the direction you want to go. Stick both poles in the snow behind you. Lift your outside ski (the one away from your poles) up, tip up, and place the tail in the snow beside the tip of the other ski. Twist your knee and ankle so you can place the turned ski next to the other one. Shift your weight to the ski you just turned, then lift the other ski, tip up, swing it around, and place it beside the other ski. Keep your legs close together as this ski comes around so your boots are not too far apart. As you bring the second ski around, swing the pole on that side around with the ski.

When you make a kick turn on a hill, remember:

1. Keep your skis pointed across the hill so neither the tips nor the tails are pointed downhill.
2. Stamp the snow a few times with your uphill ski to pack down a firm base to stand on.
3. Place the strap ends of your ski poles under your bottom and lean against them for support. The basket ends of the poles are put in the snow uphill of you.

How to Walk Uphill

Downhill skiing is most fun when you can take a chairlift to the top of a hill and ski down. Walking uphill is a lot more work, but it is important to know how to do it. The best time to learn how to walk uphill is right now, while you are learning how to control your skis.

A driver would not get into a car and drive it away if he knew the brakes and steering gear did not work. He would have an accident because he couldn't steer or stop the car. In the same

A kick turn is easy to do. Here's how: Begin by standing with both skis together.

Stick your poles in the snow behind you and uphill. Use the poles to support you by leaning against them with your hips.

Move your downhill ski up, tip up, as shown, and swing it around to point it in the opposite direction.

Place it in the snow alongside the uphill ski, but pointed in the other direction.

Swing your uphill ski around, together with your pole, to bring it alongside the other ski.

You are now headed in the other direction.

way, it wouldn't make sense for you to ride to the top of a ski slope and start down until you could steer yourself safely and stop where and when you want to. However, in order to learn to steer and stop you will have to use a gentle slope, which means walking up. Besides, uphill walking builds muscles and helps you to learn to control your skis. There are two ways skiers walk up a hill: they use the side step and the herringbone.

When you walk up a hill used by other skiers, be sure to remember this: When walking or climbing in a ski area, skis should be worn and the climber or walker shall keep to the side of the trail or slope. This advice comes from the Skier's Courtesy Code.

The Side Step: The side step is the easiest way to climb uphill. It is also the least tiring. If you pretend that you are climbing stairs, it will be easy to learn.

1. Stand with your skis together, parallel, placed across the slope so they point neither up nor downhill.
2. Dig the edges of your skis into the snow by bending your ankles and pushing your knees forward and toward the hill. The uphill edges will both bite into the snow, which will put the ski bottoms flat on the make-believe "step" you are standing on.
3. Lift the uphill ski a few inches off the snow and place it uphill, on to the next "step." Move your uphill pole about the same distance up the slope and stick it in the snow. How big a step you take will depend on your size. Take a comfortable step, six inches or so, not too far uphill.
4. Bring the downhill ski up beside the other ski. Bring the downhill pole up with the downhill ski.
5. Repeat this until you have climbed as high as you want to go. With each step, keep the uphill ski flat on the make-believe "step" you stand on. This means you will keep your knees bent forward and pushed toward the hill.

If you want to climb uphill and at the same time move across the slope, you can use the diagonal side step. It is the same as above except that you slide your skis forward a bit with each step.

(Top) The side step is the easiest way to climb uphill. Pretend you are climbing a flight of stairs sideways.

(Bottom) Move your uphill ski a few inches uphill onto the next step.

The Herringbone: While the side step is the easiest, least tiring way to climb up, the herringbone is faster. Most skiers use it for climbing quickly for a short distance up a gentle hill. You can get tired fairly quickly when using this climb. It is called the herringbone because your tracks in the snow make a pattern that looks something like the ribs of a fish.

The inside edges (the ones that are closest to each other) of your skis are important in this method of climbing.

1. Start on a flat, snow-covered surface. Spread the tips of your skis so they form a V.
2. Bend your knees and press them together. This makes your inside edges bite into the snow. Lean forward a bit. Practice walking on a flat surface.
3. Step forward with your left ski. Bring your right pole up as far forward as your left boot.
4. Repeat with the right ski and the left pole. Keep your knees bent and pressed toward each other. Keep your skis in a V. Your weight will be on the inside edges.
5. After you have practiced on a flat surface, start walking straight up the hill. Use a gentle slope for practice.
6. If the hill gets steeper, lean further forward and press your knees closer together to make the inside edges bite deeper into the snow. Pound your skis fairly hard into the snow with each step. Do not lift the skis high off the snow with each step, just high enough to lift them off the surface.

If you find that the tails of your skis are crossing, remember to move your boots in the direction they are pointed (forward and outward) rather than straight ahead.

Skiing Downhill

As we mentioned before, each time you ski down a hill, conditions can be different. The snow may become more densely packed, icier, softer, or bumpier. There may be more or fewer skiers on the slope and the slope itself may become steeper or more gentle as you ski down. This is something you will enjoy—

(Top) Here's how to climb uphill using a herringbone climb: Spread the tips of your skis so they form a V. Press your knees together so your weight rests on the inside edges of your skis (the edges closest to each other). Bend your knees, then step off.

(Bottom) When the hill gets steep, just lean forward more and press your knees even more toward each other.

finding different conditions each time and being able to meet these changing conditions.

Before we talk about the ways you can ski down a hill, let's talk about some of the words we will use in the rest of this book and some of the things you will want to know to be able to control your speed and direction.

Ski in Control: At first, you will be moving at a speed of from three or four miles per hour (m.p.h.) to ten m.p.h. As you learn more about skiing, your speed will go up to fifteen, then twenty m.p.h. or more. The secret of skiing fun is being able to stop or change direction while skiing at a safe speed. You will want to ski no faster than you safely can and your speed will depend on the slope, snow, how many others are on the slope, weather conditions, and how well you ski. Another way of saying this is "Ski in Control."

Uphill and Downhill: In Alpine skiing, we are mostly interested in skiing down a hill. Skiers use the words "uphill" and "downhill" all the time. You might talk about the downhill ski, or the uphill pole, or the downhill boot, or the downhill shoulder, even the downhill ear. It is much easier to use these words than to say "the left" ski or "the right" boot because you will be changing direction often. When you think "uphill" and "downhill" and shift your weight and position at the right time, you are on your way to being a good skier.

Except when skiing straight down the fall line, you will have an uphill ski and a downhill ski. Learn to think uphill and downhill when skiing, rather than left and right. In this picture, the downhill ski is his right ski. When he turns, though, his downhill ski will be the left one. In traversing, you must keep your weight on your downhill ski and it doesn't matter whether it is the left ski or the right ski.

Cover Your Boots: Your knees and ankles do a lot of work for you while you ski. They help you go in the direction you want, and they take up the shock of bumps and turns. They can't do this work if you keep them straight and stiff. They must bend. A good way to keep them bent enough to absorb the shocks of skiing is to remember to "cover your boots." The picture shows you what this means.

Weight Shifting: You can shift your weight in several ways: leaning (or body position), hopping up, a sudden half-squat (or drop), and stepping. The way that you shift your weight and the position your body takes will depend on what you want to do. However, you will have to shift your weight almost all the time while skiing.

    The reason for all this weight shifting is to keep the center of your body weight between your skis. However close or far apart your skis may be, or however steep or gentle the slope may be, or whatever maneuver you want to do, try to shift your weight so that it is always centered between your two skis.

Edging: Your skis have steel edges along their bottoms. When new, these edges are sharp—and they should be kept that way. You can test them for sharpness yourself. Rub a fingernail across each edge, in several places. If the edge is sharp enough, it will scrape off a bit of your fingernail. If they aren't sharp enough to do this, take them to a ski shop for sharpening.

A good way of remembering to bend your knees properly is to remember to "cover your boots." This means that you bend your knees enough so that you can't see your boots when you look straight down. When you are in this position, your weight will be forward where it belongs, on the balls of your feet.

Edges are important in skiing since they permit your skis to bite into the snow. This helps you to turn, to traverse, and do other maneuvers. When we use the word "edging" or "edging in" in this book, we mean moving or twisting your ankles and knees so that one or two of your ski edges digs into the snow. In order to edge properly, your weight must be shifted—both to allow the edges to dig in and to help you keep your balance.

Let's see what happens when you use various combinations of edging and weight shift. If, as in these pictures, you stand on the side of a gentle hill with your knees bent and your skis pointing across the slope, you can do different things by shifting your weight and edges. If your skis are flat on the hill, with no edging, you will start sliding down the hill, sideways. This is called sideslipping.

1. If while sideslipping, you shift your weight to the downhill edges, you will cause them to dig (or edge) into the snow. This will stop the ski and you will fall downhill. Not a very good idea.
2. If you shift your weight so that most of it is on the uphill edges, you will slow down and stop.
3. If you lean forward, turn your shoulders so they point downhill, then place your weight on the inside edge of your downhill ski, you will begin skiing across the face of the hill. This is called traversing.

The Fall Line: The fall line is a path down the steepest part of a hill. It is the path a ball would take if it were rolling down that hill.

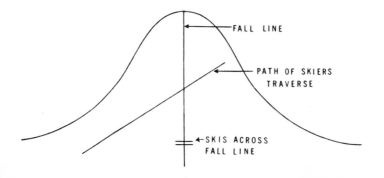

To begin a sideslip, move your knees away from the hill. This will release your edges.

This skier has begun his sideslip. Note that he keeps his knees bent and holds his hands out from his body for good balance.

He has just stopped his sideslip quickly by pressing his knees toward the hill. This causes his uphill edges to dig into the snow and stop the sideslip.

If your skis are pointed down the fall line, they would be pointed down the steepest part of the hill. If they are pointed across the fall line, they would not be able to slide, except sideways. Most skiers, except racers, ski at an angle to the fall line in what is known as traversing.

Traversing: To traverse is to ski across the face of a hill. If skiers couldn't traverse, we would be able to ski only on very gentle slopes, because we would go too fast and be out of control. We can make long traverses or short ones, shallow traverses or steep ones. In changing traverses from one direction to the other, the skis cross the fall line.

3

Skiing Down a Small Hill

After you have learned how to walk uphill and know the words used in skiing, it is time for the real fun—skiing downhill. The first lesson is skiing straight down a small slope, one that isn't steep at all.

How to Run Downhill

In skiing, the words "running downhill" mean that your skis are pointed straight down the fall line, rather than across the face of it as in traversing.

1. Choose a gentle hill for your first runs. It should have a long, flat surface at the bottom, or an upturn, so you will gradually slow down and stop.
2. Climb up the hill using the side step.
3. When you are about four or five feet higher than the bottom of the hill, stop.
4. Stick your poles into the snow, downhill, as shown in the picture. Place your hands on the top end of your poles and keep your arms straight, with elbows locked. Support yourself by leaning on your poles.
5. Starting with the tail of your uphill ski, step around until your skis are pointed down the fall line. Keep your elbows locked to keep from sliding until you are ready.

6. Your skis should be apart comfortably and your weight should be divided equally on each ski.

7. Bend your knees to cover your boots. Lean forward from the knees to shift your weight forward, over the balls of your feet.

8. Raise your poles and let yourself go down the hill, keeping your weight forward.

9. When running downhill, hold your hands slightly forward and away from your body. Point your poles backward and down, so the baskets are a few inches off the snow.

10. Look ahead to be sure that you see other skiers or bumps in the snow. Relax. Don't stiffen up.

11. If you run across a bump, bend your ankles and knees to take up the jolt.

(Top left) When you have climbed about four or five feet higher than the bottom of the hill, stop and stick your poles into the snow, downhill.

(Top right) Step around until your skis are pointed down the fall line.

(Bottom left) Your skis should be apart comfortably and your weight should be divided equally on each ski.

(Bottom right) Raise your poles and let yourself go down the hill, keeping your weight forward.

Running downhill is a lot of fun and can be used in some exciting games. You can make bridges of two poles stuck in the snow with another pole hanging from them. See who can go under the cross poles without knocking them down.

Pretend that you are a rabbit. As you run down the hill, give little hops by springing up and forward to lift the tails of your skis off the snow. See who can hop the most times without falling.

Practice running straight down the fall line several times until you can do it easily without falling and until it is fun and you are looking forward to something more difficult.

It's fun to ski under pole bridges. Duck down to go under the bridge without knocking it down, then straighten up until you come to the next one.

(Top) To skate, spread your ski tips so they form a V, lean forward, and push off with one of your skis. You will slide forward on the other ski. (Bottom left); Note how this skier keeps his knees bent and uses his poles to help push himself along. (Bottom right); As you skate, shift your weight from side to side so it is on the ski that is sliding forward.

How to Skate

Skating on skis is one way to get from one place to another on level snow. You could walk, but skating is quicker and more fun.

1. Stand with your weight evenly divided on each ski.
2. Spread the tips so they form a V.
3. Lean forward, push your right knee inward and push against the snow with your right ski. You will slide forward on your left ski.
4. As you slide forward, dig in the left ski and push, as above.

Each time you shift from one ski to the other, shift your weight to the ski that is sliding forward and use the opposite pole to help push you along.

After you have learned to skate, try a game of tag with your friends. Or have a race. Either of these games will help you to learn skating.

How to Snowplow

You can use the snowplow to slow down without changing direction while skiing straight down a hill. Learning the snowplow also helps you to learn how and why you use your edges. When you learn the snowplow turn, you will be able to make turns in whatever direction you want and will then be able to use the uphill lifts, which is a lot more fun than walking uphill.

The Basic Position: Practice this on a level spot.

1. Move the tails of your skis apart until they are about as far apart as the length of your ski pole.
2. The tips should be as far apart as the width of the basket on your ski pole.
3. Move your knees toward each other so they point to the center of the snowplow. This puts your weight on the inside edges of the skis. Keep your hips above your heels.
4. Stand so that your weight is evenly divided on each ski.
5. Hold your hands out from your waist and forward of your body, about as high as your waist.

Snowplowing down the Fall Line: Climb up a gentle hill using a sidestep.

1. When you are about five or six feet higher than the bottom of the slope, stop. Turn around, using your poles as you did when starting your run downhill.
2. An easy way of getting into the snowplow position on the hill is to shift your weight from side to side as you step each ski out. That is, shift your weight to the left while you step the right ski out, then shift the weight to the right as you step the left ski out, and so on.

58

This picture shows the proper positioning of your skis in the snow-plow position. The tips of the skis should be about a basket width apart and the tails about a pole length apart.

3. When you are in the snowplow position and are ready to snowplow down the hill, lift the tips of your poles from the snow and hold them behind you, as shown in the picture. Keep your hands about waist high, forward, and to the sides.

4. You will be sliding downhill. You can control your speed by making the snowplow wider or narrower. The wider the V is, the slower you will go. The more you push your ski tails out, the more they will bite into the snow.

5. Keep your weight evenly divided on each ski and keep them edged the same amount.

6. Lean forward, to keep your weight on the balls of your feet, by bending your ankles and knees, not by bending at the waist.

7. When you reach the flat area at the bottom, you will stop. Side-step back up the hill and practice snowplowing again.

Remember, when you want to slow down or stop, push the tails of your skis farther apart by bending your knees toward each other and pushing your heels out. One of the few times when you can shift your weight slightly backward so it is mostly on your heels is when making a snowplow stop. When you want to go faster, bring the tails closer together, making sure your weight is forward.

Whether you slow down or speed up, keep the tips the same distance apart. Make the snowplow V wide or narrow by moving the tails, not the tips.

A reminder: Stay on a very gentle hill until you can snowplow easily and the snowplow position feels comfortable and until you can turn and stop when you want to.

Look at the pictures. Notice that the skier is standing bent forward only slightly from the waist. She is not sticking her bottom out in a half-squatting position. She is leaning forward. If she leaned back, she would fall. Practice using the proper snowplow position until you can do it easily and without even thinking about how it's done.

In and Out: In and Out is a game that will help you learn to change from a straight downhill running position to a snowplow and back.

1. From the start of a gentle hill, run straight downhill with your skis a few inches apart and parallel.
2. As you gain speed, push the tails apart (Out) and get into the snowplow position.
3. As you slow down, bring the tails back together (In) and get back into the running position again.
4. As you again begin to go faster, push the tails Out again to the snowplow.
5. Pick a spot ahead of time where you want to stop. When you get close to it, spread out into a wide-V snowplow to stop.

If you will practice this over and over you will soon be able to control your downhill speed easily and can show yourself that you control your skis—that they don't control you.

How to Make a Snowplow Turn

When you know how to do a snowplow easily and can do the In and Out game, it will be time to learn how to turn.

Suppose you're snowplowing straight down the fall line. Both skis are headed downhill and neither one is the downhill ski. Yet,

This skier is ready to snowplow down the fall line. Her knees are bent and pressed toward each other. She is leaning forward and is supporting her weight with her poles until she is ready to start downhill.

She is now snowplowing down the hill. Her weight is forward and she is looking ahead, not down at her skis. Note that her ski tips are about a basket width apart and the ski tails are about a pole length apart.

you will read in this book—and you will hear instructors tell you—that to turn you should put your weight on the downhill ski.

The explanation is that to turn you should put your weight on what *will* be the downhill ski. If you are snowplowing, an easy way to remember this is to put your weight on whichever ski is pointed in the direction you want to go. So, if you want to turn to the left, shift your weight to the right ski, since it is pointed to the left.

Turning to the Left: It is best to practice making a turn first in one direction, then the other. Let's start with a left turn.

1. On a gentle slope, the same one you used to learn to snowplow, begin by snowplowing down the fall line.
2. Pull your right shoulder back a little.
3. Shift your weight to your downhill (right) ski by bending at your knees and waist. Lean to the downhill side so that your upper body is over the right ski.
4. At the same time, press your knees forward and to the left. This helps the downhill ski to edge in and the uphill ski to slide around the turn.
5. Keep both skis in the snowplow position. Hold your hands about waist high, out from your body, and ahead of you. Look in the direction you're going. Keep your knees and ankles bent.
6. Stay in this position until you make a complete turn and stop.

Practice making turns to the left until it is easy. Then practice turns to the right.

To make a snowplow turn to the left, pull your right shoulder back a
little, and shift your weight to your right ski by bending at your knees
and waist. Lean to the downhill side so that your upper body is over
the right ski.

Turning to the Right: Turns to the right require that you do the same things as turns to the left, except that body movements and weight shifting are reversed.

Side to Side: After you can make turns to the left and the right, try the Side to Side exercise:

1. Snowplow down a gentle slope, straight down the fall line.
2. Lean over the left ski, in the snowplow turn position. You will begin to turn to the right.
3. As soon as you begin to turn, straighten up into the snowplow position with your weight equally on each ski. You will start to go down the fall line.
4. Lean over the right ski, in the snowplow turn position. You will begin to turn to the left.
5. As soon as you begin to turn, straighten up into the snowplow position with your weight equally on each ski. You will start to go down the fall line.
6. Continue shifting weight from side to side like this and you will make a series of small turns.

Do not be satisfied to ski forever in the snowplow position. Running and turning with your skis close together (the parallel position) is not only more fun, it is less tiring and it looks much better. As soon as you can do a good snowplow, go on to stem turns and the more advanced turns. Think of snowplowing as being the same as learning to crawl before you learn to walk.

Tips on Turning: If you have trouble in getting into the proper body position for a snowplow turn, pretend that a little dog, about as high as your knee, is trotting alongside your downhill boot. Bend sideways and pat him on the head. Another trick is to put your hand on your side, as if you had a sideache. Or, you can lean over to hold the back of your thigh.

Here is a way of showing yourself just how much to drop your

64

downhill shoulder when making a snowplow turn. On a level spot, stand in the snowplow position. Hold your poles together in both hands, as shown. Keep both hands at the same height, just above your waist. Now, get into the snowplow turn position. As you drop your downhill shoulder, the poles on that side will point downward. You can see just how far your downhill shoulder drops by looking at the angle of the poles. They should be at about the same angle as the hill you make snowplow turns on.

When you begin your snowplow turn, remember to bend your knees forward *and* in the direction you want to go.

In heavy, wet snow, such as we have in the spring, too much edging will make turning difficult. If you ski in this type of snow, let your skis rest flatter on the surface, with not so much edging as you would use on powder or hard-packed snow.

As shown here, you should drop your downhill shoulder so that a line drawn between your two shoulders or your two hips will be at the same angle as the slope you're using for turning.

Ready for the Lifts!

Most ski areas have uphill lifts of some kind on a gentle novice slope. After you can link your snowplow turns together and stop, you will have enough control to take your first ride uphill. We will show you how to use these lifts in the next chapter.

Remember that it is easy to learn many things just by watching others and doing as they do. In fact, some young skiers have learned to ski this way. Be very careful, though, that the person you imitate is a truly expert skier, such as an instructor or a ski patrolman. You can learn a lot of bad habits by watching the wrong person.

Riding Uphill

Uphill lifts help make skiing easy. They take all the work out of getting up a slope. They should be used only by skiers who can stop when they want to and steer themselves where they want to go. If a skier cannot do this, he is probably going to get hurt, and he may hurt another skier at the same time.

Ski Area Maps: Every ski area has a map showing all the trails, open slopes, lifts, and lodges. The map might be a signboard, outside, with the trails, etc., painted on it or it might be a printed paper map, much like a road map, which is given to skiers.

Take a little time to study the area map. You will notice that the steepness of each trail is shown. Pick a novice lift for your first trips. A novice lift lets you off at the top of a gentle slope. It would be a mistake to take the wrong lift and end up at the top of a steep slope.

Lift Line Manners: Many ski areas are crowded on weekends and holidays when most of us can get away from school and jobs to go skiing. There is often a long line at the bottom of the lift. This is one of the times when good manners show on the ski area. Stay in line when waiting your turn to use the lift. Don't try to sneak in ahead of others. Stay off other skiers' skis. If you shove and fuss because you have to wait your turn, you will not have much fun and neither will your fellow skiers. When it is your turn to use the lift, move quickly. If you are not sure about how to use it, ask the operator. That is one of the reasons he is there. If an operator or attendant asks you to do something, do it. He is there to make sure that the lift runs smoothly and he is an expert at his job.

At the top of the lift, get away from the unloading area as soon as you can so the skiers behind you won't find you in their way. If you use a rope tow, a poma lift, a J-bar, or a T-bar and fall off, get out of the way quickly so you don't get in the way of the skiers behind you. Snowplow back down to the bottom again and get back in line.

Gondolas and Cable Cars

These are the luxury uphill lifts. In these, you are out of the wind and arrive at the top nice and warm. Cable cars are found mostly in Europe; however, they are now found in some areas in this country and are more and more popular. With cable cars and with some gondolas, you will have to take your skis off before you go in. The attendant puts skis and poles in a special rack, and you either stand or sit inside the car. Some gondolas are built so that you can keep your skis on—they rest on a bar outside the car and a door that extends down to about your knees is closed in front of you. Attendants at the top of the mountain open the door for you.

These uphill lifts are used for carrying skiers to the very top of the mountain. When you are a more skillful skier and can handle long trails from the top, you can use them.

Chair Lifts

Chair lifts are found at almost every ski area of any size. They have chairs hanging at regular intervals from a steel cable. Powerful engines move this cable around giant wheels at the top and

These skiers are studying a map of the ski area and planning which lifts they will use and which trails they will ski on.

bottom of the mountain and over rollers at the tops of towers going up the mountain. The chair usually holds two skiers. A safety bar is used after the skiers are seated in the chair.

Some chairlifts are hung from the overhead steel cable by one steel bar, which fastens to the center of the chair. Other chair lifts have two vertical bars that attach to each side of the chair. Here is how to get on a double chair lift:

1. As soon as the two skiers ahead of you and your partner are seated in their chair and move uphill, move quickly to the loading spot. There may be arrows or some other sign or the attendant will tell you where to stand.

2. Hold your poles together in your outside hand, the one away from your partner.

3. Stand with your skis a comfortable distance apart, pointing uphill, and turn your upper body toward the inside (toward your partner), and look back toward the chair as it comes toward you. (If the chair lift you use has two vertical bars, one on each side of the seats, you can turn to the outside.)

4. When the chair comes close, reach your inside hand back and use it to steady yourself on the vertical bar when the chair arrives.

5. Sit down quickly with your back against the chair back. Do not wave your poles around—you could hurt someone.

6. As you start to move forward, remember to keep your ski tips up to avoid catching a ski tip in the snow.

7. Pull the safety gate across in front of you and sit quietly. Rest your skis on the support bar if your chair has one.

8. Either hold your poles in your hand or hook the straps in the pole hooks if the chair has them. Do not let your poles hang below the chair. They could catch on a tree or something below you. Hold them firmly to keep them from slipping away and falling to the snow below where they might hit another skier.

These pictures show you the steps in getting onto a chair lift:

Move to the ready position when the skiers ahead of you move toward the loading spot. As soon as the chair ahead of you is loaded, move quickly to the loading spot.

Hold your poles together in your outside hand. Point your skis uphill and twist around to face the oncoming chair.

When the chair comes, sit down and enjoy the ride to the top.

Riding uphill is enjoyable. You can admire lovely scenery on the way up and can think how lucky you are that you don't have to do a lot of climbing. If you have buckle boots, you can loosen them and wiggle your toes to warm your feet.

When you near the top, here's what you do:

1. Open the safety gate and footrest. There is often a sign that tells you when to do this.
2. Hold your poles the same way you did when you got on. Keep them in front of you to make sure they don't catch on the chair when you get off.
3. Keep your ski tips up as you approach the unloading ramp.
4. When your skis touch the surface, shift your weight evenly to both skis, lean forward, and ski off the ramp.
5. Move away from the unloading area to make sure you won't be in the way of the skiers behind you.

If you are unloading on one side of the chair lift and want to cross to the other side, watch the oncoming chairs and skiers carefully. You wouldn't want to get hit by them. If the unloading area does not have a sloping unloading ramp and is flat, step or skate off to the side to be sure you're out of the way.

(Top) To get off a chair lift, raise the safety bar, raise your ski tips so they don't catch on the unloading ramp, and hold your poles in your outside hand (the one away from your partner). When your skis touch the surface, shift your weight evenly to both skis.

(Center) Slide forward and away from the chair. Some unloading ramps are much steeper than this one. If you unload on a steep ramp, lean well forward and snowplow down the ramp.

(Bottom) Move away from the unloading area right away so you're not in the way of the skiers coming in behind you.

T-bars and J-bars

While chair lifts give you a *ride* to the top, the T-bars and J-bars *pull* you to the top. T-bars pull two skiers at a time and look like an upside down T. Each skier places the crossbar of the T against his bottom and is pulled uphill. The J-bars do the same thing except that they pull one skier, instead of two. They look something like the letter J—or L. There are attendants at the loading place for both kinds of lifts. Here's how to use a T-bar:

1. When the two skiers ahead of you and your partner have started to move uphill, move quickly to the loading spot. It will either be marked or shown to you by the lift attendant.
2. Hold your poles together about halfway down the shafts. Keep them in your outside hand (the one away from your partner).
3. Keep your skis a comfortable distance apart, parallel, and pointed uphill. Your boots and your partner's should be in line.
4. Twist at your waist toward the inside (toward your partner) so you can look back and see the oncoming T-bar.
5. The attendant will hold the crossbar so you and your partner can place it properly under your bottoms.
6. Reach back with your inside hand and hold the straight-up part of the T-bar.
7. Let the T-bar pull you uphill. Keep your knees bent and your weight evenly divided between both skis. Do not try to sit on the bar. It is made for pulling, not lifting.
8. Keep your skis parallel and in the tracks made by other skiers. If you ski off to the side, you might fall, and you might make it hard for other skiers behind you to stay in line.

If you should fall while going uphill, roll off to one side, out of the way of the skiers behind you. Snowplow down the hill and get back in line for another ride up.

When you arrive at the top, here's what to do:

1. The person on the side which is away from the T-bars returning downhill can ski off first, out away from the unloading area.

2. The other skier moves out when the first one is out of the way.

If there is a downhill unloading ramp, you can snowplow down-/hill. If it is flat, you can step away or skate out of the way of the skiers behind you.

Riding a T-bar is easier if you ride with someone about your same height.

J-bars are used in much the same way as T-bars, except that they are used by one person.

1. Get onto the loading spot the same as described in the T-bar instructions. Hold your poles in your outside hand, the one away from the upright part of the J-bar.
2. Twist around from your waist and watch the oncoming J-bar. When it arrives, hold it with your inside hand and put the crosspiece under your bottom.
3. Keep your knees bent, your skis in the tracks, and let the bar pull you up the slope. Do not sit on the crossbar.
4. At the top, ski or skate away from the unloading area.

When you use a T- or J-bar, watch the returning bars carefully when crossing through them. They are the ones that have gone around the big wheel at the top and are returning downhill. You could get hit by one if you aren't careful.

The Poma Lift

The poma lift (sometimes called a platter pull) is something like a J-bar. The difference is that the steel bar that pulls you up the hill is not attached to the cable. It is hooked onto it by the attendant after you are in place and ready for your uphill trip. There is a curve at the end of the steel bar, and at the end of it is a round "platter." Here's how you use it:

1. Stand on the loading spot with your skis in the tracks, parallel, pointing uphill. Hold both ski poles in one hand.
2. Place the platter between your legs and put it under your seat.

When the person ahead of you starts to move uphill, move quickly to the loading spot. Point your skis uphill and hold your poles in your outside hand (the one away from the J-bar). Twist around to face the oncoming J-bar. As the J-bar approaches, reach back with your inside hand to steady it when it gets near.

The attendant will place the crosspiece under your bottom. Let it pull you uphill.

Keep your skis in the tracks and your poles in your outside hand. Do not try to sit on the J-bar—let it pull you up the hill.

76

3. Hold the bar tightly and let the attendant know you're ready.
4. He will put the bar on the moving overhead cable and you will start up the slope. Many poma lifts start with a jerk, so be ready, with knees bent.
5. Riding uphill is much like using the J-bar. Don't try to sit. Let the platter pull you. Be sure to keep your skis in the tracks.
6. To get off, slide your hand down the bar, spread your legs, and take out the platter. Let it go and ski out of the way.

The Rope Tow

A rope tow is a moving rope which you hold tightly to go uphill. The rope goes around two large wheels, one at the top of the slope, the other at the bottom. Powerful engines turn the top wheel, which keeps the rope moving. Use the rope tow as shown in the pictures.

Here's how you use the rope tow: Loop the straps of your poles around your outside wrist, the one away from the rope. (Top right) Stand with your skis in the tracks, parallel, pointed up the slope. Put your inside hand around the rope and slowly tighten up to get moving. Bring your outside hand behind to hold the rope. Your inside hand will be ahead and the outside hand behind you. Bend your knees. (Bottom right) Lean back and let yourself be pulled uphill.

Be careful that loose clothing doesn't get caught in the rope. It is best to wear a pair of old gloves or mittens, or gloves with tough palms. The sliding of the rope through your hands can wear out a pair of soft leather or wool gloves.

When you near the top:

1. Let the rope go with the outside hand, the one behind you.
2. When you are at the spot for unloading, let go with the other hand and ski away from the unloading area.

5

Skiing Down a Novice Slope

After you can do a snowplow, a snowplow turn, a series of snow-plow turns, and stop, it is time to ride to the top of the novice slope. If the area you use has more than one novice run, choose the one with the gentlest slope.

For your first few trips down this new slope, practice doing the same things you have been doing: make S curves down the hill with a series of snowplow turns; practice making your skis go In and Out; pick out a spot downhill from you and practice stopping at that spot.

In this chapter you will learn how to traverse, sideslip, and how to make stem turns and stem christies.

How to Traverse

To traverse is to ski across the face of a hill, rather than straight down the fall line. Therefore, it is important to learn to traverse properly. Also, the advanced turns can be made only from a properly done traverse. Here's how to get into the traversing position:

1. Stand at one side of the ski slope with your skis together, parallel, and pointed toward the other side of the slope.
2. Keep your boots together with the uphill boot about half a

bootlength ahead. Your uphill knee, hip, and shoulder will also be ahead. Pull your downhill shoulder back slightly (remember: advance everything uphill).

3. Bend your knees to "cover your boots." Press your knees toward the hill. The uphill (or inside) edge of the downhill ski will edge into the snow. Both knees should be bent at the same angle and should touch each other, with the downhill knee inside the back of the uphill knee.

4. Twist, or rotate, at your waist so your shoulders face forward and slightly downhill. Bend sideways from your waist to lean your upper body downhill. Keep most of your weight on the ball of your downhill foot.

5. Hold your hands out and forward, with your knuckles pointed toward the snow, and point your poles behind you, uphill. The tips of your poles should be a few inches off the snow (remember: keep the baskets uphill).

When you are ready to begin traversing across the slope, slide your ski tips just a little downhill, then give yourself a little push with the poles to get into motion. Bend forward from your knees, not your waist. Look ahead, in the direction you're going. If the slope becomes steeper, press your knees into the hill even more and lean your upper body downhill more.

This skier is in the traversing position.

When you reach the other side of the slope you can stop by using a snowplow stop. However, a better way of stopping can be done by sideslipping, then edging in. Here's how:

1. A few feet from where you want to stop, move your knees away from the hill so they are flat on the snow. You will begin to side-slip.
2. Then, press your knees back toward the hill, shift your weight forward a bit, and push your *heels only* downhill. Hard. This will bring your skis around so they are pointing across the hill, perhaps slightly uphill, and you will stop.

Traversing Exercises: Here is a good way of learning to keep your weight on your downhill ski: As you traverse across the slope, lift the tail of your uphill ski off the snow. Of course, your weight must be on the downhill ski to do this. Practice this exercise until it is easy to do. Hold the uphill ski tail off the snow while you count to three. You will be skiing on your downhill ski.

There are two good reasons for keeping "everything uphill advanced." First, if your uphill ski is about half a boot length ahead of the downhill ski, it will be hard for the two skis to cross. The tip of the downhill ski will prevent it. Also, you can more easily keep your weight on the downhill ski.

Here's another good exercise: As you traverse, bring the tail of your uphill ski apart from the other ski to form a half V. At the same time, bring back your uphill shoulder. Then return the ski and shoulder to the regular traverse position. Do this until it is easy to do. This exercise helps you to learn the stem turn.

If you find yourself having trouble keeping the weight on your downhill ski, try this: as soon as you cross the fall line in a turn and begin to traverse, stretch your downhill arm out and point your downhill pole down the slope. This downhill reaching not only shifts your weight downhill, it helps you to stay in the traversing position.

You can stop by making a snowplow stop, but a better way is by side-slipping, then edging in, as shown here.

How to Sideslip

Sideslipping is important in skiing. In the advanced turns, your skis will sideslip, or skid, after you cross the fall line. Before you learn sideslipping, here are a couple of words you should know: When used here, the word "release" means to make your skis lie flat on the snow so they no longer "edge" or dig into the snow. The word "reset" means to edge them in again by pressing your knees back into the hill. Here is how you can practice sideslipping:

1. Stand on a hill in the traversing position.
2. Push your downhill pole into the snow a couple of feet below you. The pole will stop your sideslip if you lose control.
3. *Slowly* bring your knees away from the hill. This will release your edges and you will begin to sideslip.
4. To end the sideslip, press your knees back toward the hill to reset the uphill edges.

Practice this until it is easy to do. Then practice going into a sideslip while you are in motion, traversing across the hill. Do not use your downhill pole to catch yourself while sideslipping from a moving traverse.

Remember the sideslip when you graduate to a steeper hill and come to an icy spot or to a spot that is either too steep or too narrow for you to make a turn.

It is fun to ski on one ski.

How to Make a Stem Turn

Think of the stem turn as putting together the traverse and the snowplow. As you traverse across the hill, you make half a snowplow V, turn, then traverse again in the opposite direction. The stem turn is another "learning turn." It helps you to learn to make the stem christie and parallel turns.

In skiing, the word "stem" refers to pushing the tail of your uphill ski up the slope to make half of the snowplow V. The stemmed ski is the turning ski because you will shift your weight to it. Here's how to do a stem turn:

1. Traverse across the slope. For practice, use a slope that isn't too steep.
2. Stem out the tail of your uphill ski. Keep the tips of your skis even and about three inches apart.
3. As you stem out, rotate your shoulders so they face uphill, as shown in the picture. Make these two motions at the same time: stem out/rotate shoulders. Keep your chin directly above the boot tip on your stemmed ski.
4. Slowly shift your weight to the stemmed ski. You will turn, across the fall line, to the opposite direction. Keep a good snowplow position during the turn.
5. After you have turned, slide your new uphill ski down beside the other one and begin traversing.

A stem turn is begun from a traverse:

Traverse across the hill with your
weight on your downhill ski.

Make two motions at the same
time: stem out/rotate shoulders.

The stem christie is another learning turn. It is the first of the skidded turns—those turns that use a sideslip or skid to finish the turn. Again, learn it with the idea that it is just another step toward making you an expert parallel skier. You do less plowing and more skidding and you do everything a little faster. Here's how to do it:

1. Traverse across the slope.
2. Stem the uphill ski out and press your knees toward each other. The ski tips should be even—neither should be ahead of the other. At the same time you stem out, rotate your shoulders so they face uphill and bring your downhill arm across in front of you.
3. Shift your weight to the stemmed ski. Sink down over the stemmed ski and plant your downhill pole about halfway between your boot and the ski tip. Use the pole as a mark to turn around.
4. Just before your skis cross the fall line, hop up and forward and move your skis into the traverse position (remember: hop across the fall line). At the same time, move the basket of your planted pole behind you.
5. Press your knees in the direction of the turn and sink down a little with your knees bent to set your edges.
6. Skid around for the rest of the turn by pushing your heels downhill.

When you made the turn, you shifted your weight from one set of edges to the other. At what time did you change these

To make a stem christie: (Top) Traverse across the slope. (Upper middle) Stem the uphill ski out and rotate your shoulders. (Lower middle) Shift your weight to the stemmed ski. (Bottom) Hop across the fall line.

89

edges? You shifted weight and changed edges during the up-hop (remember: change edges when you change direction).

When you do a stem christie or other skidded turns, heel push is important. It is the heel push that gives power to the turn. During the last part of a christie turn, press the tails of your skis around by pushing hard toward the outside of the turn.

Also important in skidded turns is the knee push. If, during the turn, you remember to push your knees in the direction you want to go, your turns will be much easier to do.

Try this to help you control the skidding around that is so important:

1. Traverse across a hill at a fairly good speed.
2. Hop up, sink down hard, press your knees toward the hill, and push your heels downhill. Hard. This will cause your ski tips to move around so they are pointed across, or up, the slope. You will stop. This is a christie stop.
3. As you stop, plant your downhill pole two or three feet down the slope.

After you can do a stem christie in either direction, it is fun to try to make one turn after the other with as little traversing between turns as possible. As soon as you finish a turn, begin another so that you zigzag down across the fall line. If you begin to go too fast, push your heels down hard after a hop across the fall line. This will slow you down.

Garlands: Sometimes, you will want to get out of the way of another skier, or a rock or a tree without making a turn across the fall line. Here's how you do it:

1. For learning this exercise, pick a smooth, open, fairly steep slope.
2. Traverse across the slope.
3. Stem out your uphill ski to form half of the snowplow V.
4. Slowly change weight to the stemmed ski. This will make you begin to turn toward the fall line.

5. When you are headed downhill, shift your weight off the stemmed ski back to the downhill ski. This will cause you to turn away from the fall line back in the direction you were originally headed.

6. Push your heel downhill to skid around and press your knees forward and toward the hill.

7. Bring your uphill ski back into the traversing position.

Repeat this exercise as many times as you can before you get to the other side of the slope. Then turn and practice it again while headed in the other direction. Making garlands allows you to move downhill without changing direction and without having to ski down the fall line. You will find them useful in learning traversing, edging, skidding, and knee action.

Where to Hold Your Arms

If, from the very first snowplow, you get into the habit of holding your arms out, away from you and in front of your body, skiing will be easier, you will be more relaxed, and you will keep your balance more easily. If your arms are kept close against your body, your timing, pole planting, balance, and turns will be harder to do and will be less smooth.

Your arms will move, along with your upper body, when turning, traversing, or running downhill. The steeper the slope, the farther out and downhill your arms will be during a traverse. Study the pictures in this book. They show the arms held in different positions depending on what the skier is doing, how fast he or she is going, and how steep the slope is.

How to Use Your Poles

Ski poles are useful for pushing yourself along, for helping you get up from a fall, for keeping your balance, and in other ways. In making stem and parallel christie turns, poles can help a lot if you use them as a marker around which you turn. Except when using them for turning, keep the baskets behind you. During a downhill run, hold the handles of your poles so that your knuckles point down toward the snow.

Sticking the pole into the snow is called pole planting. As with other things in skiing, pole planting is simple and easy to learn. Remember: turn around your pole. This means that you plant the right pole for a turn to the right and the left pole for a turn to the left. Use your wrist in planting your pole—both when you bring it forward before planting and when you remove it from the snow and move the basket back, behind you (remember: arms forward, wrist motion for pole planting). Before, during, and after the pole plant, keep your arms out and forward.

Moguls Are Fun

Moguls are bumps in the snow. They can add a lot of fun to a day of skiing. They can make turning easier and you can ski over them, around them, or up and down the same side. You can jump from the top of a mogul or you can ski over it. Skiing over and around large moguls is a good way of learning proper balance.

Knee and ankle action is important in taking up the shocks caused by skiing over uneven surfaces. It is best to practice skiing over small moguls at first, at fairly slow speeds. When you see several of these bumps below you on a slope, ski off to the side and look at them carefully. Decide where you want to go, which path you will follow. Then as you ski through them, keep your eyes ahead so you can see the next one and plan where to go.

When you turn on moguls, the tips and tails of your skis are in the air. The middle is the only part of the ski touching the snow. This makes turning easier. After turning on the top you can skid down the downhill side in the new direction. During the turn, be sure to lean well forward.

Jumping over moguls will be easier if you remember to keep your weight forward and use your poles. As you approach the top of the mogul, plant your poles and hop up into the air. Before you

(Top) Many skiers raise their knees when jumping from or over a mogul. It looks flashy and makes it seem that you're higher in the air than you really are.

(Bottom) Just before landing, lower your skis as shown here, keeping your knees bent. When your skis touch the snow again, take up the shock of landing by bending your ankles, knees, and hips.

land on the other side, lower your legs and position your skis so they are parallel with the slope at the spot where you will land. When your skis touch the slope again, crouch down by bending knees, ankles, and hips to take up the shock of landing.

Practice, Practice, Practice

If you have mastered all the skiing methods in this chapter you are well on your way to becoming a parallel skier. If you are still having a little trouble with turns, jumping, or anything else, practice. Take lessons. Try to remember that it takes more than a couple of hours to become a good skier. It takes a lot of practice and patience with yourself. Don't get angry if you have trouble. Remember that ski instructors and other experts practice all the time to make sure they're skiing as well as possible.

Take a look at all the students that go to ski school. You will see expert skiers taking lessons. Why? Because they know that they can improve their skiing by having a professional instructor tell them how.

Many intermediate skiers (which is what you are now) make the mistake of dropping out of ski school after learning the stem christie. When they do this, they often develop bad habits that take a long time to get over. Stay in school. Don't be a ski school dropout.

6

Parallel Skiing

Parallel skiers are graceful and fun to watch. Skiing parallel is almost like flying or floating down a hill. When you have learned to do the stem christie, you can go on to become a parallel skier. The reason for learning all the other steps in skiing is to get you ready to make parallel turns. Parallel turns are made with your skis close together and pointed in the same direction.

Timing is very important in making parallel turns. When you learn just when to hop (to unweight), to sink (to weight), plant the pole, and edge in—and when you understand *why* all this is done—you will be doing the right things at the right time and will find parallel skiing easy.

For learning parallel turns, the down-up-down motions are important. They are:

1. DOWN to set your edges.
2. UP to take the weight off your skis so you can turn them across the fall line and into the new direction (hop across the fall line).
3. DOWN to shift your weight to the new downhill ski for either a traverse or another turn.

Here are some exercises which will make learning to ski parallel easier:

1. Find a flat spot, away from moving skiers.

2. Stand with knees bent, skis parallel and together.

3. Hold your arms out and forward and plant your poles about a foot out on either side so they are straight up and down.

4. Sink DOWN in a crouch.

5. Use your poles to help you to hop UP and forward quickly.

6. Use this up motion to lift the tails of your skis off the snow.

7. When you feel the tails leaving the snow, move them—together—to one side, a few inches.

8. When your ski tails touch the snow again, sink DOWN. Then rise UP again and move the tails of the skis, together, to the other side.

Practice this until you feel comfortable while moving your skis together during the UP hop. Next, try the down-up-down motions on a hill.

These pictures show you how to hop between your poles on a flat spot—from side to side. This exercise helps you to get used to moving your skis together in the same direction.

97

The running hop is useful in helping you to learn to move your skis together in the same direction.

The Running Hop:

1. Pick a smooth, gentle slope.
2. Ski down the fall line with knees bent, boots covered, weight divided equally on the balls of both feet.
3. Crouch DOWN and bring the basket of your right pole ahead, ready to plant.
4. Plant your right pole.
5. Spring UP, lifting the tails of your skis and moving them a few inches to the left.
6. As you rise, move the basket of your right pole back, behind you.
7. Bring the basket of the left pole forward, ready to plant.
8. When your skis touch the snow again, take up the landing shock by crouching DOWN and get ready for the next hop.

Hop from one side to the other like this until you reach the bottom of the hill. When you have practiced this until you can do it easily, try another exercise.

This young skier has just completed the hop-between-poles course. It is an excellent way to learn the down-up-down motions that are so important in skiing.

The Hop Between Poles:

1. Use a smooth, gentle slope.
2. Plant two or three ski poles (or slalom poles, if you can get them) in a straight line down the hill about fifteen feet apart.
3. Start uphill from the poles and ski down the fall line, with skis together and parallel, heading directly toward the poles.
4. A few feet uphill from the first pole, sink DOWN, then hop UP and move the tails of your skis to the right (to turn left) to pass the pole on your right.
5. As you sink DOWN after turning, rise UP again for the next hop and change of direction so you will pass the next pole by a turn to the right, with the pole on your left.
6. Pass each pole on different sides: right, left, right, left.

You can have fun with your skiing friends to see who can pass these poles the fastest and closest without running into them. Another game you can play is the pick-up hop.

The Pick-up Hop:

1. Use a gentle, smooth slope. Leave your poles at the bottom.
2. Put three or four mittens or hats on the snow so they form a zigzag.
3. Start in the downhill running position above the mittens or hats. Ski down to the first object.
4. Sink DOWN, pick it up, rise UP and point your skis toward the next object, sink DOWN and pick it up, then rise UP for the next turn toward the third object, and continue the DOWN-UP-DOWN until you have picked up everything.

The pick-up hop is useful in teaching timing and how you use your knees in the down-up-down motions. It's also a lot of fun if you have one or more friends to do it with.

Under the Bridges:

1. Use three ski poles to make a bridge. Try to get enough poles for three or more bridges.
2. Space the bridges ten or fifteen feet apart on a gentle slope.
3. Ski downhill, with skis together and parallel, toward the first bridge.
4. As you get near the bridge, crouch DOWN so you pass under it, then straighten UP until the next bridge is near and crouch DOWN again.
5. Do this until you have skied under all the bridges.

You can also place the bridges so they form a zigzag down the slope. After you've passed under each bridge and rise UP, hop your tails across the fall line to point you in the direction of the next bridge.

Beginning Parallel Turns

When you make parallel turns, you use the down-up-down motions you have learned in the exercises described so far. During a turn, several things must happen during these motions:

1. During the first DOWN motion, your weight should be on both skis. Press your knees into the hill to set your edges. Plant your pole.

2. When you rise UP and take your planted pole from the snow, your skis carry less weight than usual. This lets you:

   a) Turn your skis across the fall line;

   b) Change the lead—that is, to advance your new uphill ski half a boot length ahead—while your

   c) Knees point toward the center of your turn (to change your edges) while you

   d) Shift your upper body over your new downhill ski to weight it.

3. The second DOWN movement helps you to re-set your edges. It also helps you to push your heels to complete the turn by skidding.

Practice making parallel turns on a gentle slope, so you can ski slowly enough to think of making the proper movements. When you can turn parallel on a gentle slope, try these turns on a slightly steeper slope.

Feet Together: You will notice that instructors, patrolmen, and other expert skiers ski with their knees and skis together. With some of them, it almost seems that their boots are glued together, no matter how steep the trail or how fast they ski.

When you practice the exercises in this chapter, you will be working toward the day when you, too, will be able to keep your skis together. It would not be a good idea, though, to try to keep them together until you have good balance and can make parallel turns easily.

At first, practice moving both skis at the same time and in the same direction. Don't worry about having them together until you have practiced enough to make a good parallel turn. You will soon find the skis staying closer and closer together.

The picture on page *105* shows a mistake many beginning parallel skiers make. Although the knees are together, her feet are

This skier displays very good form. His skis are close together, he keeps his knees bent and pressed toward the hill at the same angle, his weight is forward, he holds his hands out and forward for good balance, and he is looking in the direction he is skiing. Soon, you will be able to ski like this if you practice.

If you try to force your knees together before you're ready for parallel skiing, here's what can happen—you'll be skiing knock-kneed!

apart. This comes from trying to force the knees together before being ready for it. If you do this you will be off balance.

Weight Forward: It is important to remember to keep your weight forward while skiing. How far forward will depend on conditions and what you are doing. You should feel well balanced, which means keeping your body weight centered between your two skis. With your weight forward on the balls of your feet, you will be able to traverse and turn easily. If you shift your weight back, you will fall. The feeling you should have is that you are leading your skis, not that they are leading you.

When traversing, remember: everything uphill advanced. This means your uphill ski, boot, knee, hip, shoulder, even your uphill ear, will be forward. When you are in this position and both knees are bent, it will be easy to slip your downhill knee into the arch formed by the back of your uphill knee. You will be able to edge in both skis the same amount and your skis will stay together.

When you have learned to keep knees and skis together while traversing, try keeping them together when making a skidding stop, then while making a parallel turn. Soon, your skis will stay together almost automatically.

Control Your Edges! The control you have over your edges is important in all skiing maneuvers. When you can control your edges all maneuvers are easy to do. Practice the exercises we described in Chapter Five to help you learn edge control. Practice sideslipping until you have a feeling for the exact moment your sideslip begins and ends. Practice sideslipping on gentle hills as well as on steeper slopes. Keep your edges *sharp.*

Another exercise described in Chapter Five is useful: As you traverse, lift the tail of your uphill ski off the snow. Do this until it is automatic and you can easily keep your balance. You can even ski on one ski and make one-ski turns. Make a game of it with your skiing partner. See who can make the most one-ski turns, or which one can keep his uphill ski tail off the snow the longest.

Linked Turns: Turns that are made one right after the other are called linked turns—there is no traverse between them. To link your turns, the motions are: down, up, down, up, down, up, and so on. The second DOWN motion of the first turn will be the first DOWN of the next turn. The UP motion is begun just as your skis finish their turn and you hop the tails across the fall line for the next turn.

Making one-ski turns is not only easy, but it's fun. It is useful in teaching you to keep your weight on the downhill ski.

Glossary

Alpine skiing: Alpine skiing is that type of skiing in which we ride lifts to the top of a hill and ski more or less straight down. Techniques, equipment, and the areas used for skiing differ greatly from Nordic skiing.

Angulate: A skier angulates to counteract the pressing of his knees into the hill while traversing. Angulation consists of leaning your upper body downhill from your waist.

Arlberg strap: The Arlberg strap is fastened to your ski bindings. It is wrapped around your ski boot and buckled. It prevents the ski from escaping when your bindings release. The buckle is always on the outside of the ski.

Basket: The basket is the ring attached near the tip, or point, of the ski pole. It prevents the pole from sinking deep into soft snow when planted.

Boiler plate: When warm weather causes the surface of the snow to melt and when colder weather later causes the surface to refreeze, the surface becomes hard and icy. This is boiler plate.

Bindings: See Release bindings.

Camber: When you put skis on the floor on their bottoms, they will touch the floor at the shovels and tails. The middle of the ski (the waist) will be off the floor. The curve that is built into the ski in the middle is called camber. It allows your weight to be distributed evenly along the entire length of the ski when you stand on it. Without camber, almost all your weight would be on the middle of the ski and you would not be able to ski well.

Chair lift: A chair lift consists of chairs suspended from an overhead steel cable by steel bars. You sit in the chair and ride to the top of a ski slope. Most chair lifts will carry two skiers, although you might find single or triple chair lifts.

Check: A check is a movement, such as an edge set, which slows you down when skiing downhill. This word is also used to describe the examination of your equipment such as, "check your edges to be sure they are sharp."

Christie: A christie is a turn in which your skis are parallel when the turn is completed, as in "stem christie" or "parallel christie." The skis are skidded around during the last part of christie turns.

Corn snow: Corn snow is composed of large particles, as compared with the fine snowflakes that compose powder snow. It is usually found in the spring and is caused by melting during warm days and freezing during cold nights.

Downhill: The word "downhill" is used to refer to the relative position of your equipment and the various parts of your body while skiing. You might refer to the downhill ski—it would be the one that is down the hill, or lower than the other ski during a traverse. Likewise, you could refer to the downhill boot, knee, shoulder, or arm.

The word "downhill" is also used to describe a racing event in which skiers compete to see which one can ski downhill, over a racing course, the fastest. One skier races at a time.

Edges: Edges are steel strips set into the running surface of skis, along the edges of the skis.

Edging in: Edging in describes the process of making the edges dig into the snow. In a traverse, skiers press their knees toward the hill—or uphill. This causes the uphill edges to edge in and prevents sideslipping.

Edge release: Edge release describes the flattening of the skis on the snow. Thus, regardless of the angle of the slope, the skis are flat on the snow. This is done by moving the knees away from the hill and results in sideslipping.

Edge control: Edge control is used to describe the ability a skier has to place his edges at just the right angle, with the right amount of weighting so he can perform whatever skiing maneuver he desires. He must have a feel for the position his edges are in at any given moment, and what effect edging in or edge release will have on the traverse or turn he wishes to make.

Fall line: The fall line is the steepest path down a hill.

Garlands: A skier makes garlands when he traverses, skis downhill, traverses, skis downhill, and so on. The garland is a way of losing altitude, or getting downhill, without making a turn.

Giant slalom: The giant slalom is a racing event—usually over a rather long course—in which poles are placed at intervals down the course. The racers must ski between the poles. Whoever skis the course correctly in the shortest time wins.

Gondola: A gondola is an uphill lift which is enclosed to protect the skiers from wind and cold weather.

Heel push: Heel push is the act of pushing downhill with your heels to make the tails of your skis skid. Heel push is used when completing a christie turn or a skidded stop, or when checking.

Herringbone: The herringbone is a method of walking up a slope with skis. The tips are spread to form a V and the knees pressed forward and toward each other. The pattern left in the snow by a skier doing a herringbone resembles the ribs of a fish.

J-bar: A J-bar is used to pull skiers to the top of a slope. It is shaped something like the letter J (or L) and is a vertical steel bar suspended from an overhead steel cable. At the lower end of the vertical bar is a crosspiece.

Kick turn: The kick turn is used to change direction when standing in one spot. It can be used on a flat surface or on a hill.

Lift line: Lift line describes the lineup of skiers waiting their turn to use an uphill lift. These words are also used to describe the ski trail situated directly below a chair lift or gondola.

Linked turns: Linked turns are a series of turns made immediately one after the other. The skier does not traverse between turns. The path made by linked turns looks like several S's linked together.

Mambo: Mambo describes an advanced skiing technique in which the skier makes a series of long, linked turns, using an exaggerated movement of his upper body in one direction while his skis are pointed in the opposite direction.

Mogul: A mogul is a bump on a snow-covered hill. It may be caused by a natural bump under the snow or it may be caused by snow kicked up by many skiers turning on the same spot.

Nordic skiing: Nordic skiing is divided into two activities, cross-country skiing and jumping. Each is done with specialized equipment which is different from equipment used in Alpine skiing.

Parallel: Parallel describes skis that are together and pointed in the same direction.

Pole: A ski pole is a steel or aluminum shaft with a pointed end. Near the point is a circular ring fastened to the shaft (see Basket), which keeps the pole from sinking into soft snow when planted. At the other end is a handle and strap.

   Another kind of pole seen on ski slopes is a slalom pole. It is frequently made of bamboo. Racers in a slalom or giant-slalom race must go between certain of these poles. When slalom poles are used in pairs, they are called "gates."

Pole planting: Pole planting describes the act of sticking a ski pole in the snow. During advanced turns, skiers plant a pole to serve as a turning mark (remember: turn around your pole).

Poma lift: A poma lift is an uphill lift. Long steel poles are suspended vertically from an overhead moving steel cable. At the lower end of the poles is fastened a round disk (sometimes called a "platter"). The skier places the disk between his legs and is pulled uphill.

Powder snow: Powder snow describes light, fluffy snow.

Release bindings: Release bindings are metal devices used to fasten a skier's boots to his skis. They are designed to hold securely until too much strain is put on them, as in a fall.

Rope tow: A rope tow is a device used for pulling skiers uphill.

Royal christie: Royal christie describes skiing on one ski. The other ski is held off the snow with the tip higher than the tail.

Schuss: To schuss is to ski straight down the fall line.

Shovel: The shovel is the forward end of the ski, which is turned up at the tip.

Sideslip: To sideslip is to slide downhill sideways by releasing the uphill edges.

Side step: The side step is a way of walking uphill.

Sitzmark: Sitzmarks are holes in soft snow which are made when you fall. Be sure to cover them up, or fill them in, before you ski away.

Slalom: A slalom is a racing event in which skiers must go between slalom poles spaced at intervals down a race course. The slalom race is shorter than the giant-slalom or downhill races.
A slalom ski is one especially designed for slalom racing.

Snowplow: In a snowplow the tips of the skis are about a basket width apart and the tails of the skis are about a pole length apart. The skier bends his knees, presses them toward each other, and leans forward.

Snowplow turn: This turn is made while in the snowplow position by shifting your weight to the ski that is pointed in the direction you want to go.

Stem: To stem is to move the tail of the uphill ski up the hill to form half of the snowplow V. It is done from a traverse.

Stem christie: A stem christie is begun from a traverse. The uphill ski is stemmed out, weight is shifted to that ski, the skier hops across the fall line, brings his skis together, and skids around to the traverse or into another turn.

Stem turn: A stem turn is begun from a traverse. The uphill ski is stemmed out, weighted, and the turn begins. The snowplow position is maintained until the turn is finished, when the traverse position is resumed, or another turn begun.

Step turn: A step turn is used to change direction while standing on a level spot. A series of small steps is taken toward the direction you want to go.

T-bar: A T-bar is an uphill lift. T-bars look like upsidedown T's suspended from an overhead moving steel cable, as is the J-bar, and work the same as J-bars except that T-bars can pull two skiers up a hill.

Tail: The tail is the rear end of the ski.

Tip: The tip is the front end of the ski.

Traverse: To traverse is to ski across a hill.

Unweight: To unweight is to lessen the amount of body weight on a ski for a short time. You can unweight by hopping up, by dropping, by stepping, or by leaning. While the skis are unweighted, they are easier to turn.

Uphill: The opposite of downhill (see Downhill).

Wedeln: Wedeln (pronounced VAY-dln), an advanced form of parallel skiing, is a series of connected parallel turns, usually down the fall line. Control of the skis and movements of the body are from the waist down.

Weight: To weight a ski is to apply body weight to it. For instance, to make a snowplow turn, the skier leans over the downhill ski. This weights the ski and causes it to turn.

Recommended Reading

Casewit, Curtis W. (1968). *Ski Racer,* New York: Four Winds Press

Cavanna, Betty (1957). *Angel On Skis,* New York: William Morrow and Co.

Cooke, Donald E. (1954). *The Narrow Ledge of Fear,* New York: Nelson

Lougee, Laurence W. (1965). *Ski Champs,* New York: Pageant Press

McDonnell, Virginia (1966). *The Ski Trail Mystery,* Philadelphia: MacRae

McSwigan, Marie (1942). *Snow Treasure,* New York: E. P. Dutton and Co., Inc.

Meader, Stephen W. (1961). *Snow on Blueberry Mountain,* New York: Harcourt, Brace and World, Inc.

Miller, Helen M. (1965). *Ski The Mountain,* New York: Doubleday and Co.

Philbrook, Clem (1955). *Ski Meister,* New York: The Macmillan Co.

Styles, Showell (1960). *Sherpa Adventure,* New York: Vanguard Press

Ullman, James R. (1954). *Banner In The Sky,* Philadelphia: J. B. Lippincott Co.

Van Der Loeff, A. Rutgers (1958). *Avalanche,* New York: William Morrow and Co.

Summer Camps for Skiers

You may be interested in going to a summer camp that specializes in skiing. At these camps, you will ski every day and will be taught the finer points of skiing by real experts. Some of these instructors are Olympic champions. Some ski camps are for racers while others are for skiers who just want to have fun and improve their skiing abilities. Whichever one you choose, it would be a good idea for your parents to make arrangements very early to make sure you can go.

Mr. Franz Gabl (Mt. Baker Summer
    Ski Camp)
P.O. Box 1104
Bellingham, Washington 98225

Mr. John Hitchcock
All American Summer Ski Camp
    (at Cooke City, Montana)
P.O. Box 342
Williamstown, Massachusetts 01267

Mrs. William Larkin, Jr.
(Red Lodge International Ski
    Camp, Montana)
Box 352
Red Lodge, Montana 59068

Mr. Jim McConkey (Garibaldi
    Summer Ski Camp, B.C.,
    Canada)

Garibaldi Ski School
Alta Lake 2
British Columbia, Canada

Mr. Bud Nash
International Summer Racing
    School
Government Camp
Oregon 97028

Mr. Willy Schaeffler (Arapahoe
    Basin, Colorado ski camp)
Dillon, Colorado

Mr. Pepi Stiegler (Jackson Hole Ski
    Camp)
Jackson Hole Ski Corporation
Teton Village, Wyoming 83025